Introvert

How to Boost Confidence and Overcome Social Anxiety

Aya Chante

Table of Contents

Introduction

I want to thank you and congratulate you for downloading the book, *"Introvert: How to Boost Confidence and Overcome Social Anxiety"*.

In this book, we will explore what it truly means to be an introvert, along with the challenges that this personality type faces in their everyday lives, and how to overcome those challenges. A lot of people are not even aware that they are introverts, which leads to a lot of unnecessary stress that could be solved just by having more information. This trait is actually a great strength, and if you don't believe that, this book will convince you with plenty of evidence.

Being Introverted is not the Same as being Shy:

Introverts may be shy, but these two traits do not necessarily go together. This is a key fact to be aware of if you want to understand yourself better and leverage your personality to achieve the life you wish for. With the information given in this book, you will learn to understand yourself better, and also to take it less to heart when others misunderstand you, coming to realize how valuable your personality type really is.

Becoming Empowered by Acquiring more Knowledge:

The key to rising to your highest potential is becoming more knowledgeable about yourself. Trying to achieve your greatest dreams without being aware of what your specific gifts are is similar to having a box of tools without knowing how any of them work. So, let's go over some of the most important aspects to using your personality type to your advantage in the career field, relationships, and more.

Thanks again for downloading this book, I hope you enjoy it!

Your Free Gift

As a way of saying thanks for your purchase, Aya has made a Free companion to this book that will help you get results with regards to your purpose, finances, health and many more using the power of affirmations. Get excited, enthusiastic, and live a more fulfilling life with: *101 Affirmations Companion Guide.*

This PDF has **actionable and easy to do techniques** in a printable checklist to get the results you want.

http://bit.ly/affirmpdf

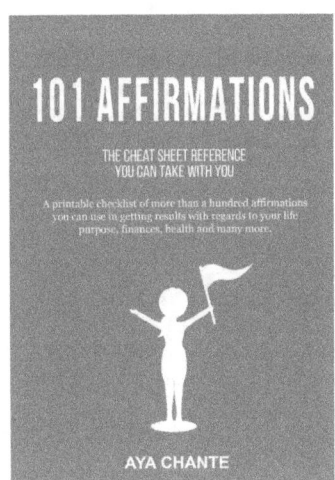

Chapter 1:

Thriving in Today's Social Noise

CHAPTER 1

Extroversion and introversion are highly misunderstood terms when it comes to psychology and the study of personality. A lot of people assume that either title describes whether you enjoy being around others or not. Although this may be true for some people, it's too simple and, therefore, misses much of the point. A person is rarely one or the other, since this trait occurs on a scale with varying degrees. However, the best way to sum it up in a simple way is this:

- **Extroverts:** Being in social situations recharges this personality type, and they enjoy stimulation that is outside of them. They tend to be outgoing, talk to others easily, and can be in crowded places without a problem, enjoying the liveliness of being around many people at a time.

- **Introverts:** Being alone recharges this personality type, and they can get easily overwhelmed by too much outside stimulation. They tend to be more reflective, often looking inside themselves for answers, rather than to others. They usually prefer to stay away from crowded places, and like hanging out in smaller groups or one-on-one scenarios with friends.

Questions to Ask yourself to Find out Whether you are Introverted:

- Do I get called mellow or easygoing quite often?

- Do I find small talk boring and pointless?

- Do I tend to ponder my thoughts before speaking?

- Do I prefer smaller groups to larger groups for conversing?

- Am I often told by others that I'm good at listening?

If most of the above questions apply to you, you fall on the introverted side of the scale. Our modern culture is very biased toward extroverted personality types. In other words, people are favored and rewarded who are boisterous and sociable. This can lead more introverted types to feel irrelevant or ignored and even to feel as though their personality type is a curse rather than a blessing. Our modern world prizes the go-getter personality type. The people who aren't afraid to go up to strangers and confidently introduce themselves without a second thought. The people who have large groups of friends to laugh with any time they want; the ones who rise to the top of the food chain in their career by aggressively chasing their goals one by one.

Feeling Negative about your Personality Type:

Watching extroverted behavior being rewarded time and time again, throughout your entire life, can definitely have a strong impact in the way you view your traits of introversion. All of this can lead the introverted personality type to feel as though they are out of place in this world, or even worse, forgotten. In fact, many introverts don't even know that there are many positive aspects to being an introvert. The good news is, there are plenty of positive aspects to being this way.

There's absolutely no reason why an introverted person cannot rise to the top and achieve greatness, just because they tend to prefer quiet settings or interactions with smaller groups of people. The idea that this is an extrovert's world is a completely mistaken idea. Some people fall on the extrovert side of the scale, some fall on the introvert side, while others are very close to the center. Maybe you have a suspicion that you are more introverted, but aren't certain. If you're unsure about where you stand, here are some questions to help you find out.

People you Never Knew were Introverts:

Emma Watson and Eleanor Roosevelt share a common trait. Christina Aguilera and Abraham Lincoln do, as well. These famous figures are introverts, just like you, and a third of the world's population. The extroverted personality type gets their fuel and energy from interacting with others socially, while introverted personalities tend to require time alone to recharge their batteries, and get overstimulated or overwhelmed when they don't have a chance to do so. These facts make it simple to assume that people who make it into the spotlight as well-known stars must be extroverted, but the fact of the matter is that a lot of the world's most famous people, both in the past and currently, are introverted.

People may believe that introverts are too shy to be in the public eye, but this is not true. They have proven themselves time and time again to make fantastic public speakers and impact large groups of people across the globe. If you are skeptical about this, the list below will change your mind. Remember that this is just a glimpse of the vast array of well-known introverts out there. The list also includes Charles Darwin, Michael Jordan, Harrison Ford, and more.

- **Bill Gates:** The well-known chairmen and co-founder of Microsoft has been described by many as an introverted person, and proof that you don't have to be loud and outgoing to be successful. Bill Gates is a great example of a person who has an introverted personality, but is not shy, and doesn't get bothered by the opinions that others have of him.

- **Abraham Lincoln:** It may come as a surprise that such an introverted personality type could become president, and is perhaps much less likely to happen today. The country of the United States once valued integrity and inner strength, even if that strength was quiet, as Abe Lincoln was. He has been described as someone who didn't need to make himself appear more superior than his fellowmen, even after he held such a prestigious title.

  The fact that Abraham Lincoln was an introvert definitely proves that it's possible to be quiet, value alone time, and also have a vast power and influence over your surroundings. Introverted people can draw a lot of inspiration and courage from this fact.

- **Christina Aguilera:** This may also come as a surprise to some, since she has such a powerful voice, but Christina Aguilera self-identifies as an introverted person. In addition to being quite small, she is also seemingly shy, describing herself as introverted, yet intense, and often misunderstood.

- **J.K. Rowling:** The famous author of the Harry Potter series is often described as an introverted and quiet person. People with this personality type usually say that they feel their most creative during alone time, rather than around other people. In fact, Rowling has stated online that her idea for creating the Harry Potter series came when she was on a train by herself on the way to London.

She had always written, since a very young age, but she had never been as struck by an idea as she was then. She was very frustrated because she couldn't find a functioning pen, and felt too shy to borrow one from someone on the train. This actually ended up being a blessing, however, since she was able to sit during an hours-long delay and come up with the details that would later on make her a famous name.

- **Eleanor Roosevelt:** She was the First Lady of the United States, for the longest period in history. This remarkable woman was famous for her entertaining, friendly, and public personality. She gave lectures, held press conferences, and served as a spokeswoman for the UN when her husband died. In addition to all of this, she was introverted. Biographies about her describe her as an awkward and shy child who grew into a woman sensitive to the needs of underprivileged people. She openly spoke about the importance of being friends with yourself before prioritizing friendships with other people.

- **Mahatma Gandhi:** Among our list of famous introverts is the incredible Gandhi. He was so shy as a young man that, when he entered his first courtroom, with hopes of being a lawyer, he ran away! He later went on to change the course of India's history forever, and will be remembered not only in that nation, but across the world, for all time.

Known for his quiet and peaceful manner, he didn't stop his introversion from allowing him to have a passionate and profound impact on his fellow Indians.

- **Audrey Hepburn:** Although she was very public when she became famous, this actress was a self-proclaimed introvert. She loved to spend time alone and also prioritized quiet walks in nature. While some might believe that extroverts are more suited for careers in performance, this certainly proves the opposite.

- **Albert Einstein:** If you ever question whether or not introverts can make a real impact or become memorable figures, look no further. Albert Einstein, one of the most famous names in history, was described as introverted. He talked and wrote widely about the power of solitude and the way it stimulated his creative ideas. He also prized imagination over all else.

- **Rosa Parks:** This may come as a surprise, due to what she is famous for, but the woman who sparked a revolution by refusing to move out of her seat on the bus for a white person was an introvert, too. Most of us likely imagined her as a bold woman, but people describe her as sweet and soft-spoken. People believed her to be shy and timid, but also courageous.

- **Warren Buffett:** He's one of the richest people on the planet and perhaps the most legendary investor of all time, and he's also an introvert. He has not succeeded despite his personality, but in fact, has enjoyed so much success because of it. While the people around him in his field were losing their cool, Buffett's calm, introverted personality prevailed as he continuously made conscious, careful investing choices. He equates success in this field with having the right temperament.

These famous personalities prove that you don't have to have specific traits to be memorable and have a great impact on others. Whether you are interested in a career in performance, acting, finance, writing, or even politics, you can do it no matter what your personality type is. In fact, as happened in the case of Warren Buffet, your introversion can end up being your greatest strength on the path to success. We will discuss more about the advantages that come along with this personality type later in the book, but first, there is something important you should know.

This Trait is not a Handicap that needs Fixing:

One major fault in our Western culture is the concept of introverted people being lesser in some way, or needing to be "louder" or "fixed". Introverts have natural qualities, such as the ability to listen closely and quietly, and a preference for being alone, and these qualities allow them to bloom in a way that is specific to them. Introverted personalities have plenty of benefits and advantages over louder extroverts, and can use these traits to excel in work, relationships, and life in general.

In this book, we will explore methods for protecting yourself against the dangers that come along with being introverted, along with ways to nurture your natural traits in a way that allows you to flourish. It is my hope that by the end of this guide, you will be well aware of how great it is to be introverted.

Chapter 2:
The Loneliness Factor

CHAPTER 2

Introverted people love to be alone. They enjoy solitude, while others may thrive on social noise and loud surroundings. Although they are understanding of others' desire to be socially active, they typically find those surroundings draining and, oftentimes, quite pointless. While others may love to engage in small talk with anyone and everyone around them, finding it fun and exciting, an introvert will likely lose interest in such an interaction quite quickly, and even be mistaken for rude, for this reason.

The Importance of Balancing Solitude and Social Activity:

Being alone is as important to an introverted personality type as water, but this longing for finding solitude in the bustle of everyday life (an important need), does have a tendency to get lonely and even become harmful after a while. In extreme cases, an introvert without any social stimulation might start acting like a bit of a hermit. They may even become afraid of social interaction if they are cut off for too long. This makes the act of balancing social life with solitude a consideration of utmost importance. In order to do this, as an introvert, there are some considerations to keep in mind at all times.

Tips for Keeping Loneliness at Bay as an Introvert:

How are introverts to know when they have gone from enjoyable solitude to fretful solitude? How much time to yourself is a bit too much time to yourself? Below will be some advice for maintaining your precious solitude, while preventing yourself from becoming isolated and lonely.

- **Stay Aware of your own Personal Reactions to being Alone:** It's important to be aware of your feelings in relation to spending time on your own. In fact, this is the most important point we will be making in this chapter. How often one can be alone and still feel satisfied and fulfilled on a personal level varies widely from introvert to introvert. For this personality type, the amount of time in solitude spent while still maintaining inner-joy and happiness can be quite considerable. Keeping a close watch on your personal emotions about how often you're spending time in solitude is a surefire way to know when the line has been crossed from peaceful to isolated.

  If you make a committed choice to stay vigilant about this awareness, keep a faithful log of the way your solitude is impacting your moods on a daily basis. Each day, rate how happy you are with your aloneness, on a one to 10 scale. At the end of each week, you can figure out the average and decide from there what needs to be changed. If you find that you score below five for your average on any given week, you can take the necessary steps to livening up your social life.

- **Make sure you Know yourself First:** This is an important pursuit for anyone, introverted or not, but it's especially important for the shy type of personality. When you are quiet and enjoy time to yourself, it can be hard to know which social interactions to choose for healthy relations. This actually becomes difficult or even impossible when you haven't taken the time to truly know yourself, first. Only once you are aware of what you value in other people can you begin to choose your friends wisely.

  Since introverts are especially impacted by the people they are around due to their high levels of sensitivity and empathy, they need to be careful about who they invest their time in.

- **Choose Friends who Appreciate your True Self:** Every introvert has the experience of being misunderstood by others. They wonder why you are being so quiet, or why you aren't interested in going to that party that everyone from school is attending. This can lead to a lot of pressure or even guilt-tripping from friends who think that they need to help you break out of your shell. While friends like this can be great to have around to challenge you to step out of your comfort zone, you should make sure that your friends appreciate you for who you are.

  Introverts can thrive around extroverted personality types, but they will probably feel most themselves around people who understand them on a more personal level. The benefit to hanging around people with a similar personality type to you is that you never have to explain yourself and will likely always feel understood and valued.

- **Put your Focus on Small Social Groups or One-on-One Interactions:** A lot of introverted personality types prefer to socialize with either small groups of people or only one other individual at a time. Since they tend to get turned off by too much stimulation, they might end up leaving parties full of social livelihood feeling stressed out, rather than energized or happy. This can be a quite noticeable shift in mood that gives them the temptation to avoid such functions in the future, much to the disappointment and lack of understanding from friends of the introvert.

  Interactions with small groups or single people at a time, however, are a great way to prevent or stave off the loneliness that can come with being an introvert, since it provides plenty of beneficial social aspects, without leading to overwhelm from too much stimulation. This gives the introvert a chance to forge deep, personal bonds with other people, which is much more valuable to them than dozens of interactions that stay on the surface.

- **Decide ahead of Time when you will Leave Social Gatherings:** It can be a highly uncomfortable situation for an introvert to go to a party (particularly one where they don't know anyone there), without having a pre-decided time that they will leave. It's just a fact that certain types of people get anxious about parties or gatherings, leading them to "flake out" on their friends, not out of any negative intentions or a lack of caring, but because they feel a genuine sense of anxiety about those situations.

A great way to assuage this anxiety about parties is to decide before you go, both to yourself and any friends you may be accompanying, the time of the evening you will be heading home. In addition to helping you prevent coming off as rude by disappearing early on in the night, the host of the party will likely be a lot more understanding when you do decide to leave. Since introverts tend to feel a sense of guilt about feeling uncomfortable at social gatherings, often due to the fact that their friends don't understand why, this will help get rid of that as well.

- **Decide upon the Amount of Social Stimulation you should have Per Week- and Stick to it:** Experience after experience of attempting to go out and socialize, only to feel an aversion to the whole scenario and end up wanting to leave soon after, can lead some introverts to being tempted into forgoing interactions with other people altogether. They may also feel overwhelmed and pressured by the sheer number of parties or social gatherings they get invited to and are expected to show up to.

A great method for finding a balance in social life and alone time (regardless of which needs more balancing), is to decide ahead of time how much social interaction you will have each week. For example, you could choose to commit to three social events each week. This means that if you haven't scheduled any events yet, you will be reminded and prompted to others and attempt to make plans with your friends or acquaintances. If you end up having a lot of invites during a certain week, this will give you the permission you need to turn most of them down and only attend the three that you are most interested in, guilt free.

- **Manage your Online Social Interactions in an Intelligent Manner:** For introverts, socializing in real life can be overwhelming and draining, making it tempting to shift their focus to socializing mostly on the internet. Going online lets you choose when you talk with people, and also gives you the control to stop when you want to stop. It allows you to feel engaged and activated on a social level, even when you are actually spending time in solitude. This is understandably an alluring prospect for many people who fit the introverted personality profile.

  However, you should try not to rely too much on your smartphone or computer for fulfilling your desires to speak to other people. It's extremely hard to truly know someone just using online chatting methods. It also heightens the risk of getting to know someone under false pretenses who may turn out completely different than you hoped for or imagined, leading you to be even lonelier than before. This is not to say that you should forgo online interactions altogether, since they can be highly valuable for you, but you should definitely make sure that this is not the only social interaction you are getting in your life.

- **Explain your Tendencies to Friends Ahead of Time:** While some introverts may feel like they receive backlash for their personality, this is often due to the fact that their friends simply aren't aware of how they feel. If you take the time to let your friends know what is going on inside of you when you want to leave a gathering early, or decline from an invite to go to a party, this will be less of a problem. Find out how to aptly describe your own feeling in relation to social situations, so that you can communicate it to your friends.

This can mean saying "I feel really overwhelmed when there are large groups of people or a lot of noise, and it makes me want to spend some time alone". Or "I need to spend time by myself in order to feel okay mentally, I hope you understand". This will help your friends to see that this is just a part of your personality and not anything against them.

All of these tips will help you to balance your alone time with your social life, helping you feel fulfilled and never overwhelmed. In order to receive more benefits from the tips listed above, start a faithful journal where you can record your thoughts and experiences. Having this record to refer back to will help you immensely with this balance.

Chapter 3:

Advantages of being an Introvert

CHAPTER 3

Every person who fits the introverted personality profile type has heard that they should stop being so quiet, or speak up more often. This can lead them to feel disheartened, but they should stop to question these commands. Why should someone who prefers to be quiet, stop being the way they naturally are? They may feel pressured by our society and the fact that they appear to favor introverts, but this doesn't need to be the case.

As we proved in the first chapter of this book, being louder or more social does not mean that you are automatically more prone to success. Introverted people most definitely have a lot to offer this world and may even rise to the top faster or more effectively than their louder and more social extroverted friends. There are some common misconceptions out there about introverts, that people without this personality type may have, in addition to the advantages that they might assume extroverts have. In fact, some experts claim that there is an ideal about extroverted personalities.

Extroverted Exercises tend to be Focused on in Schools:

Reasons for the perceived ideal for extroverts include universities and schools focusing on group projects or rely heavily on social interaction for making a grade. A lot of corporate offices enforce brainstorming sessions involving groups of employees, rather than focusing on solitary brainstorming. Due to an assumption that many have about extroverts being more primed for success, those exercises and characteristics get pushed onto everyone, including people who prefer their space and a quiet environment. But is assuming that focusing on extroverted means for success a smart way to go about things?

A Study about Working in Solitude vs. Working in a Group:

There has been some research done on the topic of working in solitude as a means for more effectively accomplishing goals. This study involved a group of violinists in Germany, and closely monitored the ability of each musician to play their instrument as related to how many hours they practiced alone, each day. The good violinists were then determined from the best musicians, and the time spent in solitude practicing made quite a difference in their skill level and adeptness. The best of the violinists practiced on their own more often than the violinists who were just good at their instruments.

The Intuitive Understanding that Introverts already have:

The study found that the group who was the best practiced close to four hours per day, as opposed to just over one hour a day in the group that was worst. This research shows that working in solitude more often leads to better results than group study. People who are naturally more introverted have an intuitive understanding of this need for a calm environment and plenty of space, giving them a distinct advantage over more extroverted personality types.

Introverts vs. Extroverts in Business and as Leaders:

Due to the emphasis placed on extroverted leaders by Western culture, many companies don't bother acknowledging leaders that don't fit that description and personality. The outgoing, confident, and sometimes arrogant leader is the personality type that a lot of businesses seek out for important positions. But these traits, although having some benefits, do not always lead to the results that are desired. Extroverted people in the workplace, for example, tend to be focused on reward-driven accomplishments, meaning that they might develop tunnel vision for their reward and become blind to negative consequences.

Decision-Making and Introverts vs. Extroverts:

To quickly sum up the science behind the phenomenon of focusing on a reward and ignoring consequences, these choices happen in between the newer brain and the older brain. The older part of the brain relies on instincts and is called, oftentimes, the center of pleasure. The newer brain has to do with decision-making on a rational level, as well as planning. In order to make choices throughout the day, these two brain parts must work together and usually do. However, there are times when these parts of the brain are in conflict with each other.

This means that whichever portion (the new or old) is sending stronger messages is more likely to prevail in the choice being made, often drowning out the other brain. According to experts, people who are more extroverted have a tendency to rely on their older brain, while introverted people tend to be better at listening to warning signals from the newer brain.

Some Potential Downfalls of the Extroverted Brain:

When leaders have a tendency to listen to the older brain too much, they may end up facing some serious backlash, including financial consequences. A 2009 study done by someone named Camelia Kuhnen looked closely at the gene responsible for regulating dopamine, which is particularly associated with extroverted personality types (who tend to be more of the thrill-seeking type). Dopamine is a chemical in your brain that is responsible for distinguishing rewards and looking forward to pleasure. This study found that looking at this could indicate how likely people were to take risks when it came to finances.

When this chemical was compared alongside serotonin (a chemical in the brain responsible for regulating mood), which introverts tend to be associated with, there was a significantly lower risk financially for those participants in the study. This study shows that there is a high correlation between risky behavior and extroverted personality types.

Introverted People can make Better Leaders than Extroverts:

People who tend to be on the quiet and solitary side can actually fit better into leadership roles, as long as they are leading the right people. Every so often, leaders who are more extroverted can stifle suggestions or insights from their team members, due to the fact that they think that they already know the best ways of doing things.
Introverted people may have a natural reluctance to lead or command those around them, so working with an insightful group will work best. In addition to this, introverted people have a higher tendency to make better listeners, meaning that they pay attention to the suggestions given to them and have a better ability to make those suggestions a reality.

Another Study that Proves the Benefits of Introversion:

In this study, done by the Business Review of Harvard, a team of researchers came up with an experiment to test how productive groups were with an extroverted leader versus a more introverted one. Participants (a group of college students) had to fold clothes for the study, as their efficiency for this was measured by the researchers. In the study, groups who had followers that were more proactive were substantially better at the task of folding shirts with a leader who was introverted. The followers were proactive by suggesting ideas for heightening productivity.

The leaders who were more introverted showed a higher tendency than the extroverted team leaders to listen to their team members and implement their suggestions successfully. The reason why these groups were more successful is because the leaders with introverted personality traits tended to listen more closely to their followers.

How to Think about These Traits:

As mentioned in the first chapter of this book, you can't have just one set definition for the introverted personality, since these traits happen on scales, rather than "one or the other". To think of these as opposite extremes is to miss the point entirely. A lot of introverts can act as though they are naturally extroverted when a situation calls for it, which is what has led researchers to extend their theory of personality to cover something that is more flexible, rather than rigid, or black and white. The reason this is being covered is because to put yourself into a box is to miss out on the dynamic wonder of the human personality.

People are not Confined to their Personality Type:

Psychology has found that most people have a certain baseline of personality traits. They can stretch from this baseline, but will inevitably return back to it. It's true that the majority of people are prone to a certain level of sociability, but this doesn't mean that they cannot stray from that when they want or need to. The bookish, quiet kid from school can end up getting the lead part in the play one year. This definition should be seen as a method for understanding more about yourself, rather than a rigid box to fit yourself into or to see as limiting.

There is no one definition for an introvert that will objectively determine the way they can or cannot act. We already saw proof of this in the first chapter, discussing famous introverts. Courtney Cox is introverted, but went on to become a famous actress in a wildly popular TV series. The same goes for Emma Watson. These stars show that there is no limit to what an introvert can do or which career they can choose to pursue.

Chapter 4:

Communicating with Others

CHAPTER 4

People with an introverted personality type may experience much of their lives feeling gravely misunderstood by the people around them, especially extroverted people. They may find that people misinterpret their desire to be alone, or even mistake them for unfriendly due to their quiet nature. Since social relationships are an important aspect of being well-rounded and fulfilled as a person, even for introverts, this is an area that should be paid attention to.

Tips for Improving Communication with Others as an Introvert:

Follow these tips to experience an improvement in your ability to communicate effectively with the people around you, no matter who they are.

- **Work on Developing a Positive Opinion of your Personality:** So many people go through life as introverts without realizing that they resent this fact. It's easy to have subconscious ideas of yourself without being aware of what they are, and living in a world that appears to favor extroverts makes this resentment almost a given. First, determine how you truly feel about your own personality. Do you see this as a flaw that you need to change? Learning how to see it more positively will help you immensely.

The best way to start with this is to work your way towards having a neutral view of your personality at first. This is not a flaw that needs to be solved. Identify what you find hard about being this way and then find ways to fix them without adding a bunch of unnecessary negativity to the equation. The only way we can have open communication and positive relations with others is if we first have a healthy, realistic, and positive idea of ourselves.

- **Be Aware of What Type of Introvert you are:** As mentioned earlier in this book, introversion is not a black or white personality trait, but more of a spectrum you can exist on. Introverts come in all shapes and sizes, but the most core factor of this personality trait is feeling recharged after time in solitude (or possible with one other close person in your life).

  Another key trait for introverts is that you typically desire to thoroughly digest information before you respond or form an opinion. This could mean that after watching a movie, you aren't sure how you felt about it overall until later on. To take another example, someone who is more extroverted may read something online and feel an urge to comment immediately after, while someone who is more introverted would rather ponder the message before deciding what to say or even how to feel about the material.

Every introverted person is different, so find advice that applies to you and feel free to disregard that which doesn't. Advice about introverts is meant to help you by talking about what is relevant to you, not by trying to tell you who you are, so keep this in mind. Only you can decide who you are on a deep level.

- **Know the Difference between Lacking Confidence and being Introverted:** People who are confident tend to have confidence in what they are capable of, as well as the fact that they will be well-received by their peers or people they don't know. If you do not have one of those specific branches of confidence, it's a good idea to try to improve that. However, don't mistake being introverted for having a lack of confidence. Being shy and being introverted are not the same thing, although one can easily be mistaken for the other and they often come together in a person.

It's perfectly possible that a person is social naturally and feels energized after being around a lot of people, but feels too shy to pursue these interests and gets mislabeled as introverted. It's also possible that someone prefers to listen rather than talk and be in low key situations rather than large social gatherings, and gets mislabeled as shy, rather than the correct label which is introverted.

- **Know Exactly what is Over-stimulating for you:** As previously stated, every introvert is different. This means that you will find different things over-stimulating, and being aware of exactly what they are is highly important. Some examples could be getting interrupted and asked questions when you are attempting to focus (on an activity such as studying, for example), being in crowded or loud places, socializing in groups, or even being asked to respond to a large volume of messages online.

  In order to maximize your mental energy and be able to function as well as possible, you need to know what your triggers are and attempt to minimize them and maximize calm and peaceful environments. You may have a friend you spend a lot of time with who has no problem being in loud places or around a lot of people constantly, but this could burn you out very quick. It's better to know ahead of time so you can take breaks or plan your days accordingly.

- **Focus on Growing as a Person:** Having a mindset of growth is believing that you are able to improve over time, instead of mistakenly assuming that you are stuck with whatever abilities you appear to naturally have. You may, for example, have a belief that you are able to improve at meeting others and networking, in general. Research has proven that when people adopt this type of attitude, they are much more likely to experience success.

Realize that there is no reason why you need to excel at every single subject. As long as you are improving every day, you will receive benefits and grow in life. Being perfect is never necessary, and even small steps each day add up to something huge over time. As long as you are growing, you are heading in the right direction, and there is always room to grow.

- **Figure out How to Live as Yourself:** What this means is seeking out ways to live and interact with society that don't involve putting on a mask or pretending to be more extroverted than you really are. There are plenty of ways to interact with others in a way that is not overwhelming, and to adjust your life for your tendency to reflect and digest. Also be aware that you need to time to think things over for a while before you make decisions or even decide how you feel.

Gaining awareness of yourself is the key here.

Become aware of when you should follow your natural way, and when you should take action to override your impulse to act a certain way. At times, it may be beneficial to take action on a social matter you've been considering for a long time, instead of thinking more, for example.

- **Know What thoughts tend to Inhibit Action for you:** Everyone has thoughts that hold them back and lead to self-defeating actions or a lack of action. This could be a tendency to focus on negative possibilities of taking action, or not taking into consideration positive possibilities. When you start to notice what your triggers for self-doubt are, you can recognize when irrational fears are holding you back from taking action in your life and communicating effectively with others.

  Being aware of this will help you live a healthy life and push your own limits, while working with your personality to enjoy the best results. Remember that being introverted is not a flaw, and can be a great ally as long as you know how to handle it.

- **Become Interested in your Own Mind:** The key to working with your introversion and excelling in life so that you can flourish, is becoming interested in your own mind's antics. Take the time to notice what makes you feel nervous and whether your fears are warranted or irrational. You may find that social situations cause you to freeze up and that frequent breaks in a social career environment may be necessary.

Being self-aware is the best way to gain understanding of what could potentially have a negative impact on your life. Once you understand how to work with your natural traits, rather than against them, you can begin to flourish in life and successfully communicate with the people close to you.

Chapter 5:

Having a Successful Career

CHAPTER 5

Again, being introverted is not a flaw in your character. Some of you may mistakenly believe that success in the career field is only reserved for the outgoing types, but this is a limiting belief that you should never have. It is perfectly possible to enjoy a successful career and even climb to the top and experience leadership positions.

In the first chapter of this book, we reviewed some incredible people who have rocked our world and made their name famous forever. What did they all have in common? They were introverted, extremely efficient influencers of a quiet nature who knew how to leverage their strengths to change the world without needing to be loud about it. Now, we are noticing that there are many ways to have an impact in the workplace of today. In fact, it appears as though the time has come for the quiet achievers to enjoy their time of recognition.

Business Trends which Show Promise for the Introverted:

- **Businesses are Getting Global:** The typical successful approach in the United States, which relies heavily on extroverted tactics and approaches work fantastically in the West world, but businesses are expanding every day. The advent of the internet has been especially helpful in allowing companies to reach overseas, and leaders who employ low-key, reflective styles for influence in business will be needed. The leadership style of the introvert is more effective throughout regions like Asia, where quiet dignity is revered.

- **Tough Competition in the Business World:** Competition grows and grows as businesses gain success, leading companies to seek employees and suppliers who can offer innovative and fresh ideas. While the stereotypical picture of success in business is the loud, persuasive, and self-promoting introvert, people these days stand out more if they know how to listen, rather than talk, and build up the people around them. This paves the way for introverts to step in and take the stage.

- **The Advent of Social Media:** It may not be immediately obvious, but introverts have great strength in business due to the upsurge in virtual relations for companies. People who are introverted tend to be attracted to social media platforms and other digital communication because it allows them to employ their great qualities and manage professional communication better. People who influence in a quiet way and also have experience with using social media and learning in general, are in a great position to be a part of the changing face of the workforce.

Now that we have reviewed some of the natural advantages you have as an introvert in the business world, we can get down to some actionable steps to excelling in your career.

How to Work Toward Success in the Business World as an Introvert:

Introverts can be extremely powerful figures both in home life and at work. The key is knowing how to leverage your special traits toward an attitude of success. Here are some key attributes to work on.

- **Gain a Positive Attitude about your Abilities:** Some people may have negative feelings about being introverted without even realizing it. You may see it as a flaw that holds you back from excelling in life. Find ways to acknowledge any difficulties you may have with accepting this fact about yourself, and discover how to work with it for the ultimate fulfillment in your job.

  As soon as you are well-aware of what you have to give to the world, you can carry your abilities with confidence, reaching the heights you always dreamed of in your career.

- **Know how to Pitch What you have to Offer:** Some introverts transform their ability to excel in the workplace and enjoy success professionally by learning how to pitch the abilities that you have. This can involve learning how to illustrate the benefits your boss would have from allowing you to move up the ladder at work, or knowing how to "sell" your traits to get a specific job.

The more comfortable you get with this, the better it will get. As soon as you have accumulated experience with pitching your traits and seeing real results from it, your confidence will soar.

- **Remember to Smile:** Plenty of research exists on the science behind the simple human act of smiling. We still don't know for sure, even after all of this research, why we smile, but it's clear that this act brings amazingly beneficial results to our bodies and minds when used often. Some scientists claim that smiling even gives us a type of high and makes us feel more confident in ourselves and our abilities.

  Even more important than this, though, in the workplace or a professional environment of any kind, knowing how to smile is a signal of confidence and assertiveness. When you smile,, it helps you, as an introvert, to come off as nicer and more approachable, upbeat, and socially adept. We could all use a habit of being in better moods day to day. This is a simple step to take, also, it just takes a bit of action and practice.

- **Follow Through:** Everyone knows that standing up straight, looking people in the eye, with your head held up show that you are a confident person. This is also a great method for making positive impressions and drawing attention (which some introverts prefer to avoid whenever possible). Studies show that the notion of communicating non-verbally, through gestures and bodily posture, makes up the biggest part of the way we are viewed by those around us.

Even more important than this, however, is the relation these body language signals have to our own self-assurance and self-respect. It's true that introverts typically don't desire to show off their traits or abilities However, they can still command appreciation from those around them and confidently assert that they have something to offer and are serious about their careers. Keep in mind that no matter how low you slouch, you will still be visible, but will appear insecure to others, especially at work. Stay aware of what your body language is communicating.

- **Speak with Authority and Composure:** Expert sources claim that in order to make a quality and memorable impression, we must stay aware of the tone we use while speaking, avoid talking too quickly, and also pay attention to our articulation. Reluctance to speak in public and enter the spotlight are situations which many introverts would prefer to avoid. However, perfecting your ability to express your thoughts is a valuable skill worth investing your time in.

Although words are a small part of communication, they are still significant in our interactions with others, and using them correctly is beneficial. Knowing how to select your phrases effectively, as well as refrain from unnecessary comments, shows other people who we are, what our company represents, and how far we are motivated an willing to go for success.

Someone who is introverted can get great at conversing by prioritizing experience and practice. Learning how to see speaking in front of others as a fun challenge rather than dreadful, and exploring opportunities for such whenever possible, will help you shine in important situations. Just like any other skill, this gets better the more you practice and consciously improve what needs work.

- **Learn how to be a Socially Introverted Person:** Some may believe that this is an oxymoron, but being an introvert does not mean you have to avoid talking to people or stay stuck to your desk all day at work. It's true that we may prefer not to engage in small talk, and that it often feels pointless, but networking at the office is a valuable part of excelling in your career.

  This will only take a couple of minutes a day and can pay off massively in the long run. The least this will do is let others know that we are there, and you may get lucky and create some lasting friendships while you're at it. If you aren't sure of how to start conversations, you can always get curious about people and ask them questions about their lives.

- **Learn how to be Flexible:** Becoming a successful introvert means knowing how to play the business game, and this involves knowing how to be flexible.

This tip may feel as though you are being advised to ignore your inner-nature, and go against all that you represent, but knowing how to blend in among others can be highly beneficial to your career.

To do this with success, it isn't necessary to abandon your principles or try to be someone else. All it has to do with is showcasing other parts of ourselves to people we work with in an effort to relate to them. To put it simply, talk to other people about subjects you already know they care about, rather than avoiding conversation altogether. You may even be surprised by how well it ends up going. This is what being adaptable is all about.

Having an introverted personality in a world dominated by the extroverted way is not easy at all. Attempting to enjoy career success in environments like this can be a hard challenge, but the good news is that we are not interacting with a static world. General opinions in our society have started to change. Studies show us time and time again that introverted people tend to be more creative, reliable, and all-around better performers than extroverted personality types.

Nurturing the "Social Introvert" Inside:

This shift is still happening, and until it goes through completely, learning how to hone some social skills that take into consideration your natural tendencies will help you get in on the benefits enjoyed by extroverts in the work place. By working on putting ourselves out there in a persistent way, we can have a positive impact on the way others view us and what we have to offer the world of business. Again, this isn't about being fake or disregarding our principles, but about learning how to apply different sides of us that we may not show very often.

The Challenge of the Workplace for the Introverted Personality:

Sure, there is a shift taking place in the world of business, but the truth is that introverted people are still asked continually to adapt to workplaces that are geared toward extroverted traits. These workplaces reward getting on stage and putting yourself in the spotlight. Organized business environments tend to support people who talk openly about their achievements, who aggressively speak their ideas first, and who dedicate lots of time to networking, rather than reflecting.

But the fact of the matter is, having influence over others has nothing to do with convincing people to agree with us or see the world the way we do. It has to do with knowing how to learn from the suggestions of other people and come up with a solution that benefits the whole. This method is perfect for the temperament of an introvert. This approach involves planning, patience, and persistence. If people believe that the only method that will work for accomplishing tasks is to take up the spotlight and speak louder than others, grand opportunities to learn, listen, and respond with thoughtfulness will be missed.

More Actionable Steps for the Career-Oriented Introvert:

Introverted people can have a lot of influence when they cease attempting to be someone they are not, and rather focus on the strengths they already have at their disposal. Here are some surefire ways to hone and make the most of those strengths:

- **Thorough Preparation:** An introvert will feel more confident about their ability to influence work decisions by improving their skills, formulating a plan and preparing thoroughly to follow through. While some situations may call for a spontaneous approach, you are more likely to excel and feel confident if you take this time to rehearse.

- **Plenty of Solitude:** The time spent alone by introverts will give them strength in the form of increased awareness of self and a strong creativity source to tap into. While others may end up feeling frenzied or even experiencing burnout from too much stimulation, the introvert knows that plenty of solitude will provide them with the strength they need to flourish at work.

- **Listening:** This is a valuable skill that comes naturally to most introverts, and helps them to establish understanding mutually and also rapport. Introverted personality types tend to be great at observing non-verbal cues from others, responding accordingly and thoughtfully, asking questions, and lending a sympathetic ear to the concerns of those around them.

- **Writing:** Quiet influencers can use this powerful ability to have an impact on others using their deep, well-thought out, and authentic arguments that will help spur others to take important action. Writing is a chance to perfect your articulation and get all of your thoughts out.

- **Utilize Social Media:** As an introvert, you will use this tool in an effective and thoughtful way, helping grow and develop partnerships, become more visible, and motivate others. Your talent with the written word will go a long way in reaching the ears of others, even those in other countries.

- **Use the Power of Conversation:** It's already been discussed that introverts tend to prefer small group interactions. This allows them to excel at focused and purpose driven talks related to work. This will help them become adept problem solvers at work, and also go a long way with winning over co-workers and working conflicts out.

If we remain open to consciously practicing our skills for influencing others at work, we can improve these abilities substantially. Not only will we grow to possess an unshakable confidence in ourselves, but we will expand our influence over multiple situations and people. This will result in ever-higher success rates, all from viewing the situation differently and presenting an alternative to the traditional model of what a successful business person looks like.

Chapter 6:

The Relationship Aspect

CHAPTER 6

Introverts who are single may feel as though they are less "datable" than other people, due to their quiet nature. They may see outgoing people getting chosen time and time again as love interests, while feeling ignored. But did you know that your introverted traits can be a great strength in the world of love and dating? In fact, with the right attitude and information, you will be doing even better than extroverts in your love life.

Introvert Strengths in Dating and Relationship-Building:

Although these focus mostly on non-platonic relations, this advice can apply to friendships as well, if that's the area you are most in need of focusing on.

- **Intuition:** Whether the situation involves someone you don't know well, or a trusted partner, intuition is a must for solid relationships. A key aspect of getting to know someone is being able to read their signals, including the ones that are not spoken but only implied with gestures. Introverted people tend to be great at reading and interpreting body language, making them naturally skilled at relationships.

  What might take an extroverted person years to learn (reading postures or facial expressions), an introvert intuits naturally about other people. They know exactly how to make another person feel truly listened to, which relies heavily on intuitive abilities. Introverts can sense the moods and needs of their loved one, creating stronger bonds and deeper trust. They will also naturally sense when to let go of a subject or when to press on.

- **Building Rapport:** People who are more introverted are great at building rapport in many different types of relations. Although some believe that introverts dislike being around others, that is simply not the case. In fact, introverts have a deep need for closeness and intimacy in their relations than more extroverted personality types.

  The typical introvert would prefer to have less friends, with a higher level of connection and understanding to each friend, than a huge circle of friends with less true connection and understanding. Communicating on the surface and engaging in small talk can be frustrating to an introvert, leading them to wonder what the point is of having a conversation that doesn't feel real. This ability to build deep rapport with others will help introverts a lot with dating.

  Since women must have comfort and trust to feel a true connection with someone, introverts will be the first choice for a lasting relationship. This may come as a surprise, but research has proven that introverts are better in some sales positions than extroverts, since they know how to foster relationships that involve patience, depth, and are long lasting.

- **Interest in Exploring Deeper Subjects:** The ability to nurture relationships that last long and reach deeper allows introverted people to get connected with others in a thorough way, even if they just met the person. While extroverted people might get stuck on surface topics such as the weather or a person's job and hobbies, introverts have no problem diving right into deeper topics, finding them compelling and interesting. These topics can be anything from values, to religion, to sexuality and morals.

- **Being Great at Listening:** There are few things that are less attractive than going out with someone who doesn't know how to listen and stop talking about themselves. Introverts are great at listening, which is one of their best qualities. They converse with other people with effortless skill and poise, seeing and interpreting the words and actions of the person in front of them with clarity and natural intuition.

Conversations between extroverts tend to be a bit more scrambled, with each participant tripping over the other's words, asking questions too quickly, and shifting topics at the speed of light. All you have to do is observe a conversation between a group of introverted people to see that each person is thoroughly listened to, and that interruptions are infrequent and immediately apologized for.

- **Natural Caring and Thoughtfulness:** Introverted people tend to be more self-aware and reflective than extroverted people. It is commonly stated that our world consists of the thinkers and the doers, and that our world has a need for both types. Having people who are more introspective and people who are action-oriented helps keep the world balanced. We need people who can aim, plan, and reflect, and those who can follow through.

In a world full of only introverts, we'd be surrounded by plenty of ideas and thought, but no concrete results. In a world of only extroverts, we would have all action and no forethought or careful reasoning. Due to the high level of thoughtfulness and self-awareness that introverts possess naturally, they are more sensitive to their surroundings and those around them. This means that they are a lot more likely to remember little details about their partner, making that person feel truly seen, heard, and valued.

- **Great at Reflecting on Themselves and Correcting Errors:** Yet another strength that introverts possess is their ability to reflect on themselves and improve, correcting errors along the way. They spend plenty of time getting to know themselves, making them extremely skilled at aligning with their true nature and living authentically. They consistently make sure that all is alright within them, and adjust accordingly if something needs work.

  In addition to this, introverts tend to be less ego-centered, since they aren't naturally drawn to impressing others or acquiring symbols of financial status. Their values are more geared toward integrity, morality, thoughtfulness, and empathy for their fellow humans, while extroverts tend to focus more on seeming interesting, being charismatic, or dominating social situations or spheres.

  Being skilled with correcting your own errors means that you will be stronger in managing relationships. Everyone makes mistakes when it comes to dating and relationships; it's just a fact of life. But introverts may find it easier to reflect, realize that they did something wrong, and openly admit this with humility. People who have partners that can admit their mistakes, apologize for them, and constantly try to do better, have happy and healthy relationships.

- **Quality over Quantity:** This can be also stated as preferring depth over breadth. People who are more on the introverted side of the spectrum enjoy having deep connections both in platonic and non-platonic relationships (quality). On the other hand, people who fall on the extroverted side of things tend to favor having a lot of friends, even if it means sacrificing depth of those relations (quantity).

  If you took a poll and asked a number of introverts how many people they consider themselves extremely close with and loyal to, they will probably name no more than five. To an extrovert, this could seem like an unthinkable number, but to an introvert, this is the perfect amount. A lot of times, an introvert will set a specific boundary to prevent having too many friends at a time.

  This makes a relationship (either platonic or otherwise) with an introvert a highly valuable affair. If they are taking the time to include you in their personal life and open up to you, it's because they really care. People pursuing a relationship with you will recognize and appreciate this trait. Whether your situation involves dating on a regular basis, or seeking a long-term partner, knowing how to start and keep connections with people will be a valuable skill to have in life.

- **Understanding the Importance of Recharging:** An introverted partner will always understand if you need to take the time to relax and recharge, which is one of the reasons why two introverts typically make a very harmonious couple. Whether you think that you are a full-on introvert or extrovert, you probably need to spend at least some time on your own.

  If you notice that you need solitude, don't be afraid to express this to your partner. Again, there is nothing wrong with you for having this need or even wishing to avoid social environments most of the time.

Remember that these are general guidelines, and that it may not all apply to your life. Our modern culture automatically associates being introverted with being shy or awkward, and extroversion being associated with confidence. A lot of introverted people enjoy being around others and being social, and plenty of extroverts struggle with confidence or even enjoy a quiet night in every so often. Perhaps you fall somewhere in the middle. Again, this is not a case of "either/or".

<u>Be Patient with Yourself and Find Someone who Values your Natural Traits and Strengths:</u>

No matter where you fall on the spectrum, having a patient attitude toward yourself and listening to your own inner-needs is very important for nurturing healthy and beneficial relationships. Only once you have nurtured a successful relationship with yourself can you be of value to others. It's also important to find a person who recognizes these traits within you and appreciates them, instead of wishing that you were different.

Chapter 7:

The Great Benefits of Living a Quiet Life

CHAPTER 7

In addition to some of the advantages we've already listed in the book, there are other upsides to being an introverted person and living a quiet life. Some introverts may fear that they are "missing out" on life around them by turning down social events or only keeping a small group of friends close to them. But more often than not, an introvert's negative fears about their lives have more to do with what others have judged, than with what they truly feel inside. That being said, what are some of the top benefits of a quiet life?

- **More Chances to be Creative:** When you spend a lot of time alone, not only do you have more ideas, but you have the quiet space needed to allow them to grow. If you are the type who spends a lot of time out with others, constantly engaged on a social level, you have less of a chance to record your ideas and set to work on them. The introverted type spends plenty of time in solitude, allowing their creative ideas to grow.

- **More Opportunity to Hone Skills:** With a less lively social calendar, you have more of a chance to master areas of life you have always desired to master. This can be anything from learning a language (or two) to getting great at an instrument. While an extrovert might see this time alone for practice as tedious and boring, an introvert can thrive within this, becoming truly talented in a shorter amount of time than it would take someone else.

- **Less Misunderstandings with Others:** When you are slower to speak or react to what others say, there are far less opportunities for misunderstandings. The introverted personality type is often characterized by an aversion to confrontation. While others might get tempted to become irritated easily or lash out at others due to a misunderstanding, the introvert is more likely to step back, ponder, and *then* respond.

- **You Create your own Meaning:** Spending a lot of time in solitude means that you are free to create your own meaning in life. Constantly being surrounded by the noise of other people can influence our minds considerably, and we may find ourselves "catching" ideas that we never wanted in the first place. A person who isn't afraid to be along has the power to construct their own life philosophy and live strongly by it, rather than being swayed by the opinions of others.

  However, you should be careful not to get too caught up in your own ideas that you forget how to consider the ideas of others. We are, after all, social creatures and missing out on this type of interaction and influence means missing out on amazing opportunities to learn and grow.

- **Less Reactive and Impulsive:** Introverts are more likely to pause and think in most situations, meaning that they are a lot less likely to make rash or impulsive decisions. Some decisions cannot be taken back and can have lifelong consequences, so this is a valuable trait to have. When you are a quiet person, you're less likely to get into trouble or find yourself in compromising situations.

- **People may Find you more Trustworthy:** Who would you rather tell your secrets to; a person who seems loud and outgoing, or a quiet person? Introverts make great, trusted friends, especially because their quiet nature makes them less likely to tell the secrets of others. Instead of simply speaking without thinking, they always pause to ponder their words before speaking. This makes them appear more trustworthy to other people.

- **You Feel Life more Deeply:** When you talk less, you feel more. Introverts tend to be highly perceptive and sensitive people, meaning that they experience life in a rich and complex way. Although this can be overwhelming for them, depending on the situation, it's also a great strength to have. This is one of the reasons why introverts make such great artists.

-

- ## The Benefits of being Perceived as Shy or Quiet:

- People generally experience their lives mostly through their eyes, as compared to the rest of their senses. As soon as someone meets you, they will be looking at you. This will then lead to them making a judgment about what they see, if these can be said to be two separate things. This isn't a bad thing. We all judge what we see and also get judged by other people on a regular basis. It isn't just how we appear physically that people make assumptions about us, but how they see us acting that they are paying attention to and drawing conclusions from. All people try to gain an understanding of the people around them. This is a mechanism for survival that evolved along with us, and an inescapable part of being a human being.

•

• The positive aspect to this is that you can affect the way you look to other people in order to influence the way they will feel or think about you. One of the most beneficial ways to be perceived, although it is very misunderstood and even underrated by most, is being introverted or shy. Being someone who is shy, or even just being perceived that way when you really aren't, has a lot of positive aspects to it.

•

• **You Possess an Element of Mystery:** No one can resist a mystery. People who are mysterious intrigue us, making us wonder what's going on in their inner-world. People who speak less are lot more likely to be seen as mysterious individuals, which is beneficial for a few different reasons. As said before, it creates an air of intrigue, drawing the focus of other people seemingly without even needing to ask for it. In addition to this, it lets people fill in the mystery with their own imagination. Imagination is powerful, and if you engage the imagination of others, you will find them constantly being drawn to you.

At times, you may find that people's imaginings of you were completely off base, but don't let this bother you. The fact that you are drawing in the interest of others enough for them to create these ideas of you is something that should be taken as a compliment! It can actually be quite fun to find out about all of the different ideas people will craft in their minds about the type of person you are, and if they're wrong, you can always correct them later.

- **It Gives you a Chance to Observe, rather than just Talk:** Our surroundings can be highly distracting and easy to become caught in when we constantly try to be a part of what is going on. But if we know how to take it slow, watching the action from the side, we can start to have a deeper perception of reality, having access to insights that may have been invisible to us before.

This is highly beneficial, whether you're watching while taking part in a conversation, or whether you're just watching what is happening all around you. This opens up a whole new world; a world that is full of great things, that many people don't stop to notice. The insights we can draw from our observations can lead us to a deeper understanding of both ourselves and others. Knowing how to pay attention to small cues that may have otherwise been missed will give us the insights we need to have fruitful relationships, respect others on a deeper level, and more. When someone is more perceptive, they are naturally more intelligent.

- **Most People Assume you're Good at Listening, and it's Typically True:** Since you are an introverted person, you might stay away from most conversation altogether. But when you are engaged in a conversation, you will probably find it quite interesting, especially if you aren't used to it and it's out of the norm. Being great at listening is a highly important aspect of fostering strong bonds with others, since they feel valued by you.

  Being quiet gives others a chance to open up, and when someone is talking to a quiet person, it can lead to interactions that are more meaningful, since the other person feels like you care. When someone feels as though you care about what they are saying, they're more likely to listen to you and care themselves.

- **More Chances to Know Yourself on a Deep Level:** Most of us are pretty talkative, even if it's just in our heads and we aren't saying anything aloud. People who are less chatty with other people tend to take time to talk to themselves more often, creating a healthy relationship with their inner-self. It can be easy to lose track of your own needs when you are always around other people and their antics. When you are introverted, you're better at knowing when you need time to yourself.

Everyone needs personal time, but some are better at taking it than others. Since introverts spend plenty of time on their own, they are better at successfully identifying this necessity and following through with it.

- **Less of a "Need" for Social Stimulation:** Extroverts not only feel stimulated by social interaction, but may feel, at times, empty without it. This is actually a weakness, since we can't be around people all the time and it's healthier to know how to be alone. Having a need for anything can create an unhealthy dependence, and it's too easy for such things to become a crutch or a distraction.

- **Quietness can be seen as Kindness by Many People:** Whether it's true or not, people who are perceived as shy are often assumed to also be nicer people. They are viewed as more loyal and less self-centered. Making friends with an outgoing person who is chatty with nearly everyone they meet makes the relation feel shallower, since you know that they act like that with everyone.

Making friends with a person who doesn't seem very social, on the other hand, will lead you to expect that they will be more appreciative of your interactions. You might also expect that they would be more honest. Although this depends entirely on the person, and may not always be true, people seem to feel less threatened by quiet people, putting their guards down and opening up easier.

- **Some Specifically Seek out Shy Partners:** That's right, being introverted might actually help your dating life. While some people seek out colorful, loud, and outgoing partners, other people prefer people who fall on the opposite end of the personality spectrum. Many shy people mistakenly believe that they have less of a chance at love, but that doesn't have to be true. Once the initial interaction has happened, your introversion might be precisely what your love interest has been seeking in a partner. As mentioned earlier, no one can resist a mystery.

- **When People know you're Quiet, they won't Expect Socialness from you:** Another benefit to being perceived as shy or introverted is that people won't pressure you to be social as often, or expect it from you. This is a great reason to refrain from talking to people you don't feel like talking to. The best way to avoid having talks you would rather not have is by people believing that you are quiet. If someone believes you're introverted, they won't get offended by your quietness and will also be understanding of your lack of socialness.

This can be an enormous blessing to an introvert, since one of the most uncomfortable situations is being pressured into being social when you don't feel like it.

CHAPTER 8

Conclusion

Thank you again for downloading this book!

I hope this book was able to help you to see your personality type in a new, positive light. This is a trait that should make you feel empowered instead of disheartened, and with the information in this book, you should be well on your way to making the most of your personality type.

The next step is to choose the tips within this guide that resonated most for you and get to work on them. Don't forget that keeping a journal about your experiences will help you a lot along the way. In this, you can record your intentions for the week (for example, to have three social interactions), and your success with them, adjusting your goals accordingly. There is a lot of power in being an introverted person, and this guide should have shown you exactly how.

Finally, if you enjoyed this book, then I'd like to ask you for a favor, would you be kind enough to leave a review for this book on Amazon? It'd be greatly appreciated!

Thank you and good luck!

Your Free Gift

As a way of saying thanks for your purchase, Aya has made a Free companion to this book that will help you get results with regards to your purpose, finances, health and many more using the power of affirmations. Get excited, enthusiastic, and live a more fulfilling life with: *101 Affirmations Companion Guide.*

This PDF has **actionable and easy to do techniques** in a printable checklist to get the results you want.

http://bit.ly/affirmpdf

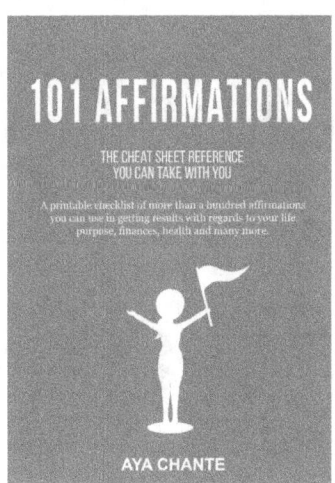

www.ingramcontent.com/pod-product-compliance
Lightning Source LLC
Chambersburg PA
CBHW060202290526
45789CB00003B/1125